Simone Bertrand and Sylvette Lemagnen

Honorary Keeper of the Bayeux of the Bayeux Tapestry

Keeper of the Bayeux Tapestry

The Bayeux Tapestry

"How extraordinary it is that while so many solid buildings have crumbled away,
this fragile strip of cloth has reached us intact across centuries,
revolutions and all kinds of vicissitudes!"
Théophile Gautier, *Quand on voyage (When travelling)*, 1865

Photographs : Ville de Bayeux
Translation: Atlantique Traduction

ÉDITIONS OUEST-FRANCE
13, rue du Breil, Rennes

The birth of a masterpiece

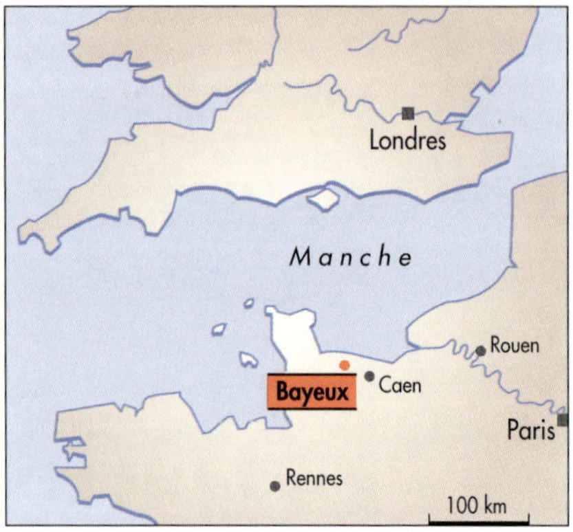

Most probably begun the very day after the famous Battle of Hastings (14 October 1066) which made Duke William of Normandy the new King of England, the Tapestry was finished at some time in the subsequent ten years. It is thought that it was exhibited for the first time on 14 July 1077, to decorate the nave during the dedication ceremonies for Bayeux Cathedral.

This magnificent building had just been rebuilt. One of those fires which so frequently ravaged the towns of the Middle Ages had almost completely destroyed the original church around the middle of the 11th century.

Bishop Hugo II, who had begun its reconstruction, died in 1049. Already aware of the importance of maintaining his grasp on spiritual as well as secular power, Duke William succeeded in having his adolescent half-brother, Odo of Conteville, appointed Bishop.

During the years which followed, the Bishop of Bayeux unfailingly lent William his powerful support and made judicious directives in his favour.

We will also see him helping William and fighting at his side during the English campaign. Immediately after the Conquest, a grateful William made him the Earl of Kent, showering him with favours.

The possessor of an enormous fortune, Odo was well able to demonstrate his generosity, in particular by deciding to pay for the complete reconstruction of the Cathedral from his own resources. In his county of Kent, he had admired the sumptuous wall-hangings which decorated holy buildings and, in planning celebrations of a great magnificence for the consecration of his cathedral, he may well have had this brilliant idea: to have one of these embroidered hangings made to decorate it, with the intention of both glorifying the exploits of Duke, now King, William, and of justifying them.

The Council of Arras (1025) had just ruled that it was desirable to adorn the walls of churches with wall-hangings depicting people, as a means of enlightening the worshippers. While the illiterate popular masses could thus learn "through

Scene 35
William and Odo

Queen Matilda

The "Bayeux Tapestry" is still frequently called the "Tapestry of Queen Matilda".

In the 18th century, when the scholarly world discovered it, Lancelot, a member of the Academie des Inscriptions et Belles-Lettres (dedicated to the encouragement of historical learning) wrote a paper on the subject (1730) and Dom Bernard de Montfaucon made the first complete reproduction of it. They both described it under the name of "The Cloth of Duke William". According to tradition, Lancelot wrote, "it was Matilda, Queen of England, Duchess of Normandy, who wove it herself with her ladies-in-waiting." Matilda embroidered the feats of her husband, taking pleasure in "depicting, in a work of her own hands, the most brilliant achievement of the life of Duke William."

Alfred Gaillard, oil on canvas: "Queen Mathilda embroidering the Telle du Conquest"
(Photo: Baron Gérard Museum, Bayeux)

From this charming legend, which made the Queen into a Norman Penelope, came the name given to the tapestry in the 19th century: the "Tapestry of Queen Matilda".

More recently, efforts have been made to restore the name formerly used by the canons of the cathedral to describe it, "Telle du Conquest" (Cloth of the Conquest). Common practice is increasingly and justifiably to call it the Bayeux Tapestry, so linking the work itself with the name of the town where it is kept and for which it is a source of renown.

the pictures", the literate and the clergy would find in addition inscriptions which commented on the pictures.

So, while the cathedral was being built stone by stone, skilled hands were working on the long wall-hanging which would explain to the Normans, in this very cathedral, how and why William had become, by right, the King of England.

It is more or less certain that it was Odo who ordered, and even supervised, the making of the Tapestry. He composed the subject matter skilfully. The Tapestry is not simply a retelling of the Conquest, it has a completely different viewpoint: the observance of a vow sworn on holy relics. Harold, the Saxon pretender, having taken an oath on the holy reliquaries from Bayeux Cathedral to recognise William as King of England on the death of King Edward, did not have the right to accept the crown for himself as he did. The breaking of this oath was the pious pretext for going to seize Edward's throne by force.

The Tapestry is an embroidery!

The first written mention of the Bayeux Tapestry known to us is found in *L'Inventaire des richesses de la cathédrale (the Inventory of the Cathedral Treasures)*, dating from 1476, where it is described as follows: "A long and narrow cloth arras with embroidered pictures and inscriptions representing the conquest of England, which is hung around the nave of the church during the Feast Day of the Relics and the week thereafter."

This is a very brief but also an exact description. In effect, this old term "arras" or "wall-hanging" is a more precise name than the most inappropriate one of "tapestry" which is usually used for a large woven work with an unbroken surface.

In reality, it is undoubtedly an embroidery "of pictures and inscriptions" the use of which, furthermore, is carefully indicated: it was to be hung from pillar to pillar, as a decorative hanging in the nave of Bayeux Cathedral. Finally, its subject is well-defined: to present the account of the Conquest of England for viewing by the worshippers.

On a background of fine-textured linen fabric, embroidered using coloured wool, are depicted the characters, the horses, the boats and all the domestic or fantastic animals which animate this work and bring it so much realism and life.

Relation of the facts is skilfully divided into scenes, sometimes edged by an outline drawing of a building, palace or seigneurial manor, sometimes by trees with foliage symbolised by beautiful interlacing, the design of which is reminiscent of the rich Irish illuminations. The historical subject occupies the centre of the cloth (covering approximately 33 to 34 cm) and is edged by two historiated borders, each measuring between 7 and 8 cm in height, curiously embroidered with pairs of animals face to face or dragons spitting fire. There is also a scene of a bear master fighting with his animal and fables from Aesop and Phaedrus.

△ *Scene 12*

◁ *Scene 9*

Motifs bordering the scenes.

◁ *Scene 4*
The fox and the crow.

Technical description

The dimensions of the Tapestry are exceptional, even spectacular. While it is only 50 cm high, in contrast it measures nearly 70 m in length. For a long time it was thought that it was composed of eight pieces stitched together. Recent scientific observation has demonstrated that there are nine, of varying lengths. The longest measures 13.9 m and the shortest 2.43 m.

The various colours employed highlight the extraordinary relief effect achieved by using two very simple embroidery stitches: a couching stitch, known as the Bayeux stitch and a stem stitch which was used for all the outlines as well as all the facial features, the hands, legs and inscriptions. Also noted are the rarer presence of a split stitch executed with double thread and a chain stitch. The latter is only found in places where restoration has occurred.

Eight shades of wool - blues, greens, reds and a tawny yellow - combine in a more or less arbitrary fashion to give a delightful perspective effect. The cloth background, left completely bare, accentuates, through the slightly brownish tint of the linen, the richness and the originality of the colours.

The Bayeux stitch

This is executed in three stages. A number of threads, tightly packed, practically one on top of another, are stretched

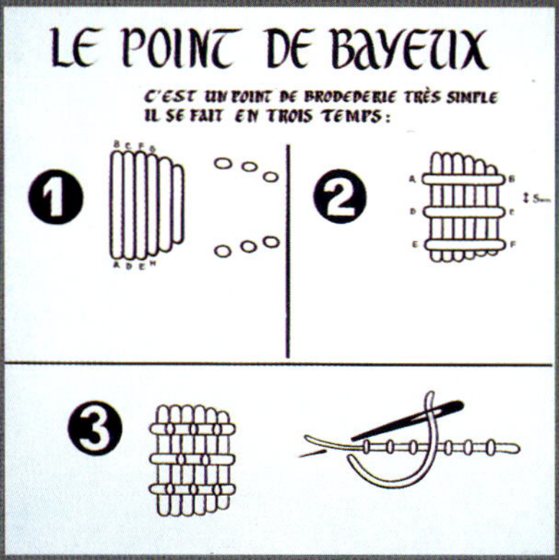

▷ ***The Bayeux stitch***

This is a very simple embroidery stitch. It is done in three stages:
❶ Covering the surface to be embroidered the front of the work is covered only tiny stitches appear on the reverse.
❷ Stretching threads at right angles to the first ones. These threads are spaced at intervals of about 3 mm..
❸ Fixing the work in place using small stitches in staggered rows.

Photo: Municipal Library, Bayeux

using a laid thread technique. The surface thus obtained is then covered perpendicularly by another set of threads spaced out at intervals of approximately 3 mm. Finally, from place to place, the length of the latter, small stitches fix the whole to the cloth.

▷ ***Fragment of the upper frieze of scenes 55-56 of the Bayeux Tapestry, front, use of the Bayeux stitch. Photo: Municipal Library, Bayeux***

Photo: Municipal Library, Bayeux

▷ ***Reverse side of the same fragment.***

Photo: Municipal Library, Bayeux

The Tapestry, a work unique in the world

This extraordinary embroidered document is the only one of its kind which has reached us through the many trials of nine centuries, and in spite of its relative fragility.

Several narrative wall-hangings from the 9th to the 13th centuries, preserved in Sweden and Norway, have been compared with it.

We mention here the tapestries of Overhogdal and Skog, found in the north of Sweden and exhibited today in the museums of Ostersund and Stockholm respectively. They too were first created in the form of a narrow band, several metres long. It seems that the former related episodes from the Sagas and the latter was of religious inspiration.

Of the Baldishol hanging, displayed at the Museum of Decorative Arts in Oslo, there remains only a fragment, of which the large size (about 2 m long by 1.70 m wide) has nothing in common with that of the Bayeux tapestry or the Swedish tapestries. It depicts bucolic figures symbolising April and May.

The wall-hanging in the church at Hoylandet, kept at Trondheim Museum, is also similar to the Bayeux Tapestry. A fragment measuring 2.14 m long by 44 cm wide depicts the procession of the Three Kings.

Finally, a small piece of embroidery belonging to the collection of the Oslo University Museum which originated from the church at Ron shows a battle: a rearing horse, warriors in agony, worked exactly like the characters in the Bayeux Tapestry.

Quite different, the "veil" of St. Martin, a work of Icelandic origin now kept in the Louvre Museum, recounts the life

Partial view of the gallery in which the Tapestry is exhibited.
(Photo: Jean-Yves Labartette)

The "veil" of St Martin, embroidered altar cloth, Iceland, 13th century.
(Photo: RMN)

of the saint in scenes which are not linked, but are executed in couching stitch.

These Nordic relatives are joined, curiously enough, by the famous wall-hanging from the cathedral at Gerona in Catalonia (Spain): *The Creation of the World*. In the borders which frame it, as in the Bayeux Tapestry, there are figures which are astonishingly lifelike, though the technique employed is completely different.

There were undoubtedly other large hangings containing figures which related scenes from the lives of the saints or the exploits of great leaders, but the Bayeux Tapestry remains the only large embroidered narrative hanging from the 11th century.

The lost tapestry of Adèle de Blois

In about 1100, a poem by Baudri de Bourgeuil described the scenes on sumptuous narrative hangings depicting the Conquest of England. They adorned the chamber of Adèle de Blois, daughter of William the Conqueror. In spite of some differences at the beginning, the description is practically identical to the story on the Bayeux Tapestry, from the building of the fleet up to the battle. But the poem also relates the procession to London and William's coronation.

The inheritance of a crown

8

The question of the succession to the English throne arose in 1064. King Edward, already old, and childless, was worried: who would succeed him as leader of this England which he had tried to govern wisely and even liberally? To appease the Saxons he had married Edith, the daughter of one of them, and welcomed to the Court her brother, Harold Godwinson.

As the years passed, Harold's ambition gradually became clearer: encouraged by the Saxon faction of which he was the popular leader, he sought no less than the crown of England on the death of his brother-in-law.

A great-nephew of Edward the Confessor would probably also put himself forward as a claimant: the young Edgar Athling. A colourless character, he

Scene 1
King Edward receives his brother-in-law Harold.

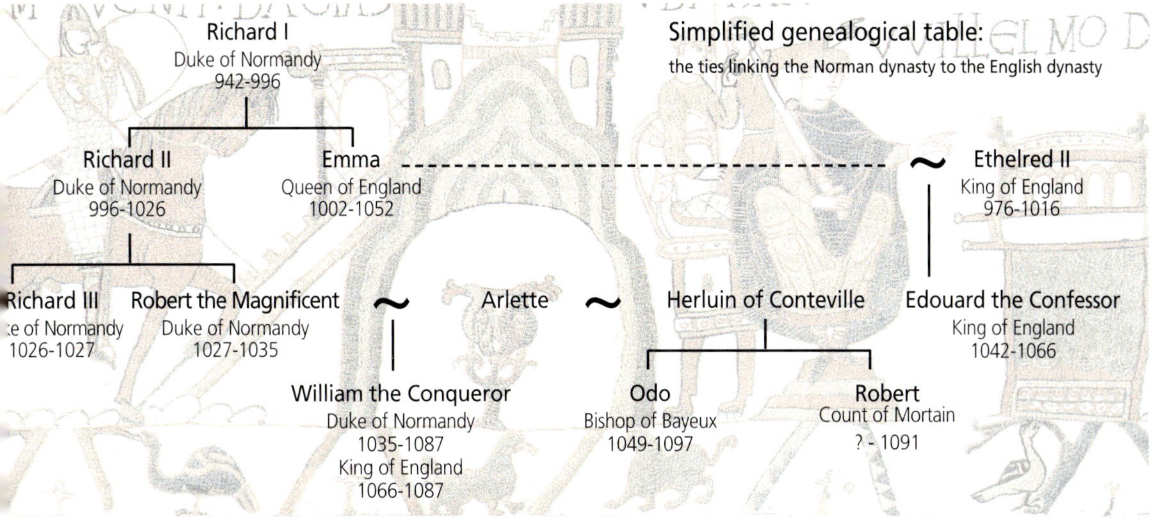

was a poor rival, all the more so because, having been brought up in Hungary, he had very few supporters.

Alongside these two claimants a third had appeared: Duke William of Normandy, second cousin of King Edward. There were those who said that, during a visit to England in 1051, Edward had already promised him the crown as a reward for the help William had given when he himself ascended the throne.

Edward had already secretly made his choice from among these three candidates. Called back to reign in 1043, following a long exile in Normandy, he had retained his Norman customs, he spoke Norman French, his entourage was Norman: he knew and liked William. William was the one he was going to name as his successor.

To put a stop to Harold's claims, the King asked Harold himself to go and give the news to William. Harold no doubt found it politically expedient to accept and set off for Normandy.

This (according to the Norman theory) is the starting point for the Bayeux Tapestry.

The story as it is related on the Tapestry

1 - Eadward(us) rex (King Edward).

In that year 1064, King Edward of England receives his brother-in-law Harold Godwinson at his palace (probably the one in Winchester). During the conversation he asks him to go to Normandy to let his cousin Duke William know that, in the absence of a direct heir, he has chosen him as his successor.

2 - Ubi Harold dux Anglorum et sui milites equitant ad Bosham (In which Harold, Duke of the English, rides to Bosham with his men-at-arms).

Harold no doubt finds it politically expedient to accept and rides, surrounded by his companions, in a peaceful procession to the south coast of England. The expedition has the appearance of a pleasant hunting party, Harold at the head, falcon on wrist, surrounded by the baying of his pack of hounds.

3 - Ecclesia (a church).

But Harold knows the dangers of the sea crossing and pauses in his journey at the small church at Bosham to pray, with his equerry, for "a calm sea and a favourable wind".

4 - Hic Harold mare navigavit (Here Harold sets sail).

The story is told quite simply as an illustration of everyday life. Everyone arrives at the manor house, where, in the Great Hall, they feast gaily while waiting to embark. This is a feast which bears the hallmarks of the recent Viking heritage: while Harold drinks from a cup, his companions use horns. A servant rushes in to tell them that they must take advantage of the rising tide; removing their hose, they walk bare-legged to the ship which the sailors are already casting off.

Scene 2

Scene 4

5 - Et velis vento plenis venit in terra(m) Widonis comitis (And, the sails filled by the wind, he runs aground on land belonging to Count Guy).

Harold's prayers were in vain: the wind which fills the sails is a stormy wind and the ship is blown off course. Instead of landing on the shores of Normandy, they are thrown onto the inhospitable territory of Count Guy de Ponthieu. Should they throw out the anchor? From the top of the mast, the lookout sees a troop of armed men approaching them.

Scene 6

6 - Harold.

Harold stands in the prow of the boat and tries to explain the reason for his shipwreck, but to no avail.

7 - Hic apprehendit Wido Haroldu(m) (Here, Guy takes Harold prisoner). The Count of Ponthieu intends to make the make the most of his

Scene 9

The players

The tapestry depicts 626 figures of which 15 are named, the most important being:
Edward the Confessor (1005-1066), King of England from 1042.
Harold Godwinson (1022-1066).
William of Normandy (1028-1087). Became William I, King of England. Better known as William the Conqueror.
Odo of Conteville (1036-1097).
Bishop of Bayeux. Earl of Kent after the Conquest.

seigneurial rights over shipwrecks. He has quickly guessed the high rank of the person to whom he is speaking from the richness of his clothes and the size of his ship and orders his men-at-arms to seize the shipwrecked company. Two solid Picards take Harold away without allowing him time to put his hose back on.

8 - Et duxit eum ad Belrem et ibi eum tenuit. (And he takes him to Beaurain where he holds him).

With a good-sized escort, the Count of Ponthieu takes Harold and his men to their place of captivity: Beaurain Castle.

9 - Ubi Harold et Wido parabolant (There, Harold and Guy begin negotiations).

As soon as he arrives in the Great Hall, an audience chamber represented symbolically by two pillars with capitals, Guy takes his place on the throne and, sword held high, discusses with Harold the size of the ransom he plans to receive before releasing him. Supported by his faithful equerry, Harold appears dismayed by these demands which he will find impossible to meet... unless he asks Duke William for help. A servant, partly hidden behind a column, furtively creeps away: probably in the pay of the Duke, he will waste no time in letting him know of Harold's imprisonment.

10 - Ubi nuntii Willelmi ducis venerunt ad Widone(m) (In which Duke William's envoys came to see Guy).

Turold (Turold).

William of Normandy is about to enter the scene. No doubt he had some ulterior motive in sending two messengers to the Count of Ponthieu. Standing, leaning on his battle-axe, the latter listens to them with an air of arrogance, but behind him, his equerry is advising him to listen to the conditions they are laying before him. Even the horses, being held by the bridle by a sort of bearded dwarf, the enigmatic Turold, seem impatient.

11- Nuntii Willelmi (William's messengers).

Two envoys from Duke William set off for Beaurain again on horseback at a gallop. Armed with swords and lances, they are carrying their shields high.

12 - Hic venit nuntius ad Wilgelmum ducem (Here, a messenger comes to find Duke William).

It is with an attitude both humble and imploring that the Saxon (the man with a moustache) appears before William. The Duke listens to him, seated in his lordly apparel and immediately gives urgent orders to two men-at-arms (we know from other sources that he was agreeing to pay the ransom: a fine castle on the borders of the Duchy and the lands which belonged to it!).

12

Scene 12

13 - Hic Wido adduxit Haroldum ad Wilgelmum Normannorum ducem (Here, Guy takes Harold to William, Duke of the Normans).

Having obtained satisfaction, Guy de Ponthieu hurries on horseback to appear before William. The two armed escorts meet on the border of the Duchy. Mounted on a mule, half-turned towards Harold, the Count of Ponthieu points him out to William.

14 - Hic dux Wilgelm cum Haroldo venit ad palatiu(m) suu(m). (Here, Duke William accompanied by Harold, returns to his palace).

The Norman escort has turned round. Harold is now the guest of the Duke of Normandy who invites him to his castle at Brionne. William of Poitiers adds:

Scene 14

"There, he treated Harold and his men with great hospitality, trying to help them forget the trials of their journey: William had every reason to rejoice at the arrival of this important guest, who had come to him as a messenger from his closest and dearest friend." He accords him a solemn audience and by all appearances they have an animated discussion. Is Harold relating the story of his shipwreck? Is he speaking of the mission on which Edward has sent him? Is not William stating his formal intention to assume the crown of England on Edward's death? A prudent diplomat, the Tapestry remains silent, but on the border above the scene, two peacocks, one of which is fanning out his tail, symbolise the two leaders.

15 - Ubi unus clericus et Aelfgyva (Here, a cleric and Aelfgyva).

Skilfully compensating for the possible deception of Harold, it is stated that William offered him his eldest daughter in marriage. Under a portico, a graceful young girl, in an attitude of prayer, is being slapped gently by a tonsured cleric. This gesture can be interpreted as confirmation of the betrothal.

Scene15

Scene 16

16 - Hic Willelm dux et exercitus eius venerunt ad Monte(m) Michaelis (Here, Duke William and his army came to Mont Saint Michel).

Harold joins William to go and bring help to Rivallon de Dol, who had risen against the Breton, Count Conan II. Surrounded by his men-at-arms, William crosses the Couesnon above Mont Saint Michel, recognisable from its church built on the rock. Beside the horsemen wearing their chain mail and helmets with nasal (nose-piece), the rank and file are in simple tunics.

Scenes 19 and 20

17 - Et hic transierunt flumen Cosnonis. Hic Harold dux trahebat eos de arena (And here, they crossed the river Couesnon. Here Duke Harold pulls them from the quicksand).

In the great curves of the quicksand, men and horses are in danger of sinking and Harold, who is leading the way, courageously saves two of them single-handed (the Tapestry, a courtly work, thus pays homage to his chivalrous action).

18 - Et venerunt ad Dol et Conan fuga vertit - Rednes (And they came to Dol and Conan fled - Rennes).

While the Normans were preparing to attack Dol, the Bretons and Conan himself left the town, concealing their retreat under rows of shields. Conan succeeded in reaching Rennes, but pursued by the Norman cavalry, he had to flee the town again and seek refuge at Dinan.

19 - Hic milites Willelmi ducis pugnant contra Dinantes (Here, Duke William's soldiers are attacking Dinan).

Having succeeded, by wheeling round, in forcing the Bretons to shut themselves up in Dinan, which was vulnerable owing to its wooden fortifications, William lays siege to the town. While the horsemen are attacking the drawbridge, two soldiers set fire to the stockade with their firebrands.

20 - Et Cunan claves porrexit (And Conan handed over the keys).

Conan, beaten, must surrender: he hands over, on the point of his lance, the keys of the town to his conqueror. This marks the end of the Breton expedition.

21 - Hic Willelm dedit Haroldo arma (Here William armed Harold).

Duke William wishes to honour Harold for the bravery he has shown during the battles and is going to "award him arms" (knight him). The new Norman knight, holding in his hand his lance which carries a pennon with four streamers, is receiving from the Duke's hand the helmet with nasal, the coat of mail and the sword ... Henceforth he is William's liegeman.

22 - Hic Willelm venit Bagias (Here William came to Bayeux).

And everyone is returning to Bayeux. The town is portrayed by its castle and by the two eagles which later became the arms of the cathedral chapter: the two-headed eagle. The Tapestry here provides a valuable piece of information: it was definitely at Bayeux that an event of major importance took place (though a Norman historian, Ordéric Vital, places it at Rouen and William of Poitiers at Bonneville-sur-Touques).

Scene 23

23 - Ubi Harold sacramentum fecit Willelmo duci (There Harold swore fealty to William).

What could be called a long prologue here reaches its climax: William, seated on his ducal throne, his sword raised, has had two reliquaries brought in. One of them certainly contains the bones of the martyrs Raven and Rasilph, kept in Bayeux Cathedral. One hand on each of them, Harold is more or less forced to swear fealty. The witnesses to this scene, obviously very attentive, are emphasising by their posture, by their facial expressions, their raised index fingers, the gravity of this sacred undertaking...

What is it in fact? Here again, the Tapestry is silent. Harold will now be formally bound to recognise William as the legitimate successor to King Edward and to give him assistance, both political and material, on the latter's death.

Scene 25

24 - Hic Harold dux reversus est ad Anglicam terram (Here Duke Harold returned to England).

Bound by this fateful oath, Harold can now return to England, "showered with gifts... and accompanied right to the shore by William, who is advising him once more to keep his promises well" add the Norman Chronicles; he even crosses the Channel on a Norman vessel. Over there, on the shores of England, the lookout spies the great ship, with its shields hung on the gunwales. The faces of the curious appear in the windows of a house.

25 - Et venit ad Edwardu(m) regem (And he came to see King Edward).

Hardly have they set foot on English soil than Harold and his faithful equerry jump onto their horses and set off for an unknown destination, perhaps London or even Winchester. Harold is in a great hurry to relate the story of his journey to King Edward. The hunching of his shoulders skilfully conveys the despondency of the young Saxon nobleman. Seated on his throne, the old king welcomes him with a weary face, already lined by illness.

Scenes 26 to 28

26 - Hic portatur corpus Eadwardi regis ad ecclesiam S(an)c(t)i Petri ap(osto)li (Here the body of King Edward is carried to the church of St. Peter the Apostle).

The scene showing the funeral rites oddly precedes the death of the king. The designs may have been inspired by some funeral lament.

And here, carried to the Church of St. Peter
The body of King Edward who has just died
Surrounded by his people during his agony

Westminster Abbey had only just been finished at its consecration to St Peter the Apostle had been celebrated on 28 December 1065. Above the nave, the hand of God, so beautifully modelled, symbolises this recent consecration, as does the workman about to place the weathercock on the church.

Wrapped in a rich shroud, Edward's body is carried on a litter by eight men of the royal household, the little choirboys ring their handbells, clerics and prelates sing the funeral service.

27 - 28 Hic Eadwardus rex in lecto alloquit(ur) fideles. Et hic defunctus est (Here, King Edward, from his bed, speaks to his people. And here, he is dead).

While a servant supports the old king in his death-throes, at the foot of the bed a woman weeps (Queen Edith?). The king once more finds the strength to speak with the priest who has not left his bedside and with Harold who will swear later that Edward named him as his successor when in extremis. On 5 January 1066, while a priest recites the last rites, two servants prepare him for burial.

29 - Hic dederunt Haroldo corona(m) regis (Here, they gave Harold the King's crown)The very day after the funeral, the Witangemot (assembly of nobles) decides to offer Harold the crown of England. It is then that without hesitation and despite the oath he has sworn, Harold accepts.

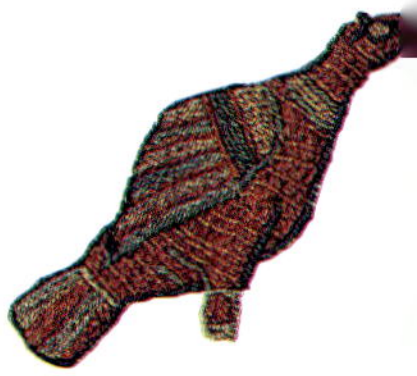

30 - Hic residet Harold rex Anglorum (Here sits Harold, King of the English).

Harold is now King of England. He will reign under the name of Harold II. Seated in majesty on the royal throne, his brow encircled by the crown, he holds the sceptre and the orb, the insignia of royalty. His vassals, swords held high, come to pay him the traditional homage.

Scenes 30 and 31

31 - Stigant archiep(iscopu)s (Archbishop Stigant).

Stigant, Archbishop of Canterbury, has just, according to some historians, performed the ceremony. Others in contrast contend that it was presided over by Alfred, Archbishop of York, but Stigant having been excommunicated by the Pope, his presence here adds to the charges against Harold.

32 - Isti mirant stella (These men are looking at a star with astonishment).

Outside the palace, six men, very frightened, have noticed in the sky a great ball of fire with a blazing tail. It is Halley's comet which was visible in England between 24 April and 1 May 1066.

33 - Harold (Harold).

A man-at-arms runs to tell Harold about this terrible omen. Struck with anxiety, he has a presentiment, even a vision, of a fleet (a ghostly fleet is faintly silhouetted in the lower border).

34 - Hic navis anglica venit in terram Willelmi ducis (Here, an English ship entered Duke William's territory).

Some men arrive from England and tell Duke William both of the death of King Edward... and of the coronation of Harold.

35 - Hic Willelm dux jussit naves edificare (Here, Duke William is ordered ships to be built).

William immediately holds a meeting with his half-brother, Bishop Odo of Conteville, whose advice he clearly seeks. A man of the church with a subtle mind, endowed with remarkable intelligence, Odo finds the answer immediately. Harold must be punished, the "punishment must be taken to the perjurer", a fleet must be built to invade England. Orders are given straight away: the length of the Norman forests, trees are falling under the axes of the woodcutters, carpenters are planing the planks, shipwrights are pegging the joints on the ships.

36 - Hic trahunt naves ad mare (Here, the ships are pulled towards the sea).

Within a few months, the invasion fleet is ready: the ships launched by a whole system of pulleys and ropes line up along the shore.

37 - Isti portant armas ad naves et hic trahunt carrum cum vino et armis (These people are taking arms aboard the ships and here they are pulling a cart loaded with wine and arms).

Nothing can be forgotten in an expedition like this. Chain mail, swords, helmets, are all loaded on board. To make things easier and to lighten their cart, the men are working in twos to carry a coat of mail strung on a pole (each one weighed between 14 and 15 kg). Others are transporting a rustic cart loaded with a barrel of wine.

38 - Hic Willelm dux in magno navigio mare transivit et venit ad Pevensae (Here, Duke William crossed the sea on a great ship and landed at Pevensey).

By the middle of August in the year 1066, the whole fleet is gathered at the

mouth of the Dives and in the neighbouring ports, but William waits in vain for a favourable wind. To calm the impatience of his troops, he tacks the ships to Saint-Valéry, at the mouth of the Somme... and waits for several weeks more... Finally, on 27 September, the south wind begins to blow and the Duke gives the order to set sail without delay. Horses and horsemen hastily board the heavy transport ships, surrounded by their light "patrol boats". The handsome ducal vessel, the Mora, a gift from Duchess Matilda to her husband, carries, at the top of its mast, the cross blessed by Pope Alexander II. William wished to give his expedition the character of a "crusade" long before the term existed.

How many ships and how many men crossed the Channel like this? The figure generally accepted is 400 ships, a considerable number for the time, and 8,000 to 10,000 men: lords, valets, men-at-arms, fishermen who joined in large numbers with their boats... (with a view to pillaging!).

On Michaelmas Eve, (St. Michael is patron saint of Normandy), 28 September 1066, the Normans land at Pevensey, a small Sussex port. The ducal ship had gone so far ahead that at daybreak it was alone. William must have been extremely worried... Then the lookout announced one sail, two sails... the whole fleet!

Scene 38

Scene 39

39 - Hic exeunt caballi de navibus (Here, the horses are coming off the ships).

Soon everyone is busy loosing the rigging, taking down the masts or leading the horses onto the shore. The landing proceeds without hindrance. Harold, thinking it was now too late in the year for such an expedition, had "demobilised" the coastal guard several weeks previously and most importantly, he and his soldiers were now occupied with an invasion (Norwegian, this time) on the north-east coast of England, near York: William had cunningly opened a "second front".

40 - Et hic milites festinaverunt Hestinga ut cibum raperentur (And here, the soldiers rapidly make for Hastings in search of supplies).

The horsemen gallop across a countryside deserted by its inhabitants and the foragers plunder pigs, cattle and sheep. In the distance a few humble peasant houses, open to the elements, seem to have walls made of horizontal planks of wood.

41 - Hic est Wadard (This is Wadard)

This knight is one of the few characters indicated by name. Already dressed in his chain mail and armed with his lance, Wadard, tenant of the lands owned by Bishop Odo, has the job of steward and organises the food supplies. He is speaking to a man who is holding a pack pony by the bridle.

42 - Hic coquitur caro et hic ministraverunt ministri (Here, the meat is prepared and the servants are carrying out their duties).

Two cooks are busy cooking meat in a cooking pot hung from the andirons and another, using a utensil with pincers, is taking the food out of a field oven. The roast chickens and the skewered meats are being given to the table servants.

43 - Hic fecerunt prandium et hic episcopus cibu(m) et potu(m) benedicit (Here, they have prepared the meal and here the Bishop has blessed the food and drink).

At a table made from trestles and some shields, the steward is having the dishes

Scene 40

Scene 43

Scene 44

set out and, blowing a horn, a servant is calling the guests to the feast. Everyone takes their place around the High Table, which is in the shape of a horseshoe. At the centre, Bishop Odo, always recognisable by his tonsure, blesses "the food and drink". To the right of the Bishop, William is half-hidden by a bearded figure: probably Roger de Beaumont, nicknamed "Roger the Bearded", whose bravery during the Battle of Hastings caused him to be mentioned by all the contemporary historians. The guests have knives in front of them, the only cutlery used at the time and the Bishop has a magnificent fish: care has been taken to show that he would have abstained from meat on 29 September, which the Gregorian calendar places on a Friday (a day of abstinence).

44 - Odo eps. Willelm. Rotbert (Bishop Odo. William. Robert).

Straight after the meal, the Duke holds another meeting. He presides at the centre, sword held high, questioning Odo, seated at his right. Robert de Mortain, his sword already unsheathed, is ready to carry out orders.

45 - Iste jussit ut foderetur castellum at Hestenga ceastra (He orders a fortification to be built in the camp at Hastings).

During this meeting one of the first decisions taken was certainly to build a sort of fortified redoubt in which to take refuge in the event of a surprise attack by the enemy. While one of the command-

Scene 45

22

ers supervises the work, labourers are busy digging ditches around one of these "wooden castles" invented by William himself and the materials for which formed part of the ships' loads. Two navvies brandish their spades, ready to sort out some quarrel between them.

46 - Hic nuntiatum est Willelm de Harold (Here, William is brought news of Harold).

In a rich residence near the camp, a messenger announces to William that Harold has just won victory at Stamford Bridge over the Norwegians and his brother Tostig, and decided to set off on a forced march to Hastings to attempt to drive the Normans back into the sea.

47 - Hic domus incenditur (Here, a house is burned down).

William does not intend to allow himself to be surprised by the enemy and gives orders for a tall Saxon manor house which is blocking visibility to be set on fire. A woman holding a child by the hand flees her burning home: "They symbolise here the widow and orphan, eternal victims of war". This is the third and last woman to be depicted in the central scenes of the Tapestry (the two others being Aelfgyva and Queen Edith).

48 - Hic milites exierunt de Hestenga et venerunt ad prelium contra Haroldum rege(m) (Here, the soldiers have left Hastings and gone to fight King Harold).

Leaving the town of Hastings, William has an equerry bring his battle horse: a superb Spanish stallion of which he was very proud and which had been given to him by King Alfonso of Aragon. The Duke, already prepared for battle, has put on a magnificent coat of chain mail, very well-designed from the point of view of protection because a chain mail hood protected the skull under the helmet with nasal. The streamers or flying ribbons on the helmet enabled the horsemen to recognise their leader in the middle of the mêlée. When his equerry slipped it on him, he put it on backwards. Seeing the appalled face of the servant who saw in this a bad omen, William just laughed.

In the shelter of a small wood, the entire Norman cavalry is grouped behind the standard-bearers. One of them brandishes a semi-circular banner, fringed and decorated with a dove, that of Robert de Mortain, the other has the Duke's standard: the famous "cross standard". (The Norman Chronicles relate that William tried then to avoid a bloody confrontation: he sent a monk from Fécamp, Friar Margot, to carry a message to Harold reminding him of the oath he had sworn on the relics and even offering him a man-to-man combat in which the judgement of God would pre-

Scene 49

vail. Harold refused: the kingdom, he contended, having been granted to him by Edward himself on his deathbed.)

49 - Hic Willelm dux interrogat Vital si vidisset exercitu(m) Haroldi (Here, Duke William asks Vital if he has seen Harold's army).

William is at the head of his troops. He is holding the commander's staff which will remain his only weapon throughout the battle. Immediately behind him is Bishop Odo whose heavy three-headed mace would cause "muche" deaths among the combatants: as a priest, he was not in fact allowed to spill blood by the sword but "clubbing to death is not as bad as slicing in two"! The knight Vital rides to meet them on his horse at a gallop. His index finger pointing at Telham Hill, he informs the Duke that the Norman advance guard has seen the Saxon army.

50 - Iste nuntiat Haroldum rege(m) de exercitu Willelmi ducis (This man is announcing the approach of William's army to King Harold).

From the other side of the wood, a Saxon lookout spies the first Norman horsemen: he turns round straight away and runs in haste to warn Harold: "The Normans are here!" King Harold, practically standing in his stirrups, makes sure of the exact position of William's army (it has been calculated that at that point about 1500 m separated the two armies). Dawn breaks, the decisive battle is about to begin: victory will decide the fate of the kingdom.

51 - Hic Willelm dux alloquitur suis militibus ut prepararent se viriliter et sapienter ad prelium contra Anglorum exercitu(m) (Here Duke William addresses his soldiers, exhorting them to be ready to fight courageously and with wisdom against the English army).

Early that morning, William had been to mass and taken communion: the whole Norman army attended the service conducted in the open air by Bishop Odo.

About to face the enemy, William, in accordance with the practice of the day, is making the customary leader's speech. He exhorts his troops to fight bravely, but with wisdom (this should perhaps be

Scene 50

translated as with discipline). The historians, William of Poitiers among others, and Henry of Huntingdon, relate his eloquent speech. William asserted that the English had never been able to resist invaders, that under his blessed banner they were all fighting for a just cause and that "if beaten there would be no hope or retreat possible for them; as the victors, the glory and treasures of England would be theirs". He was still speaking as some of the Norman horsemen set off at a gallop on their horses.

William's army did not just contain Normans, but also Bretons, men from the Maine, Poitou, the Boulogne regions and mercenaries, really adventurers, recruited from all over the place, even from across the Rhine. They were formed into three columns. The right flank, the least vulnerable, was composed of French, Flemish and mercenaries; the left flank contained all the men from Brittany, Maine and Boulogne under the command of Roger de Montgommeri and the Breton Count Fugan. William, Bishop Odo and Robert de Mortain held the centre with their Normans "having undertaken to be ready to help the other two if required". The archers marched at the head of the three sections, their great bows stretched and their heavy quivers stuffed with arrows. Next came the horsemen, all dressed in chain mail, the head well protected by a helmet with nasal. In their left hands they held their great shield, which ended in a point (like an almond) and in the right their sword or battle lance.

A few kilometres away, opposite the Normans, Harold regrouped his army at the top of Senlac Hill. Knowing that his troops were tired, he has had them take up a strictly defensive position. He had established his command post at the centre, on the high plateau with his

Scene 51

most trustworthy men, his housecarls (or royal guard), guarding the standard. They still carried Danish weaponry, the famous long-handled battle-axe with its murderous blade, and spears. The flanks were held by men of the "fyrd" or militia - troops of peasants, many more in number than the royal guard which numbered little more than a thousand men. All were to fight on foot: Harold had resolved to wait for the enemy to attack and unlike the Normans, the English rarely used their horses in battle.

"Then the terrible sound of trumpets resounded in each of the two camps

announcing the start of the battle" (William of Poitiers).

The Norman archers, flexing their bows, begin to attack, opening the way for the horsemen, but the English, well entrenched behind their wall of shields, were victorious in resisting the attack. After a terrible fight, pushed back on all sides and rebuffed by the difficulty of the terrain, they were forced to retreat.

52 - Hic ceciderunt Lewine et Gyrd frates Haroldi regis (Here fell Lewine and Gyrd, brothers of King Harold).

There are many dead on both sides and the Normans have claimed two notable victims: Harold's two brothers, Lewine and Gyrd. They had exhorted their brother in vain not to enter the battle. The entire lower border now depicts the appalling battlefield, littered with corpses, severed heads and broken swords.

53 - Hic ceciderunt simul Angli et Franci in prelio (Here, the English and the French died together in the battle).

To strengthen his position, Harold had had time to have a deep, marshy ditch at the foot of the hill fortified by filling it with sharp stakes, in the Roman manner. In their turn, the English attack so violently that the French left flank gives way and retreats in disarray and the Norman horsemen become trapped in the incredible tangle of horses sinking into the marshy ground. Men perish, crushed by their mounts. That blood-stained ditch still bears the name Malefosse.

54 - Hic Odo eps baculu(m) tenens confortat pueros (Here, Bishop Odo, holding the staff, encourages the combatants).

Seeing the Normans routed, the English come out of their entrenchment, in defiance of Harold's orders. The centre, held by William, begins in its turn to give way: panic is overtaking the Normans. It is at this point that Odo, aware of the danger, raises his commander's staff very high: he deliberately acts as leader. His rapid intervention rallies the runaways who, turning round, rejoin the battle.

▷ *Scene 53*

▽ *Scene 54*

ANGLI ET FRANCI INPRELIO

CULU TENENS CONFOR
TAT PUE ROS

55 - Hic est Willel(m) dux (Here is Duke William). **E(usta)tius** (Eustace)

The role of the Bishop of Bayeux was even more decisive in that at the same time, to complete the demoralisation of the Normans, the rumour spread that William had been killed. Standing in his stirrups, the Duke tips back his helmet and, half-turned on his horse, shows himself to his men: "Look at me now, I am truly alive, and God willing, I will be victorious!" Near him, Eustace of Boulogne, his standard-bearer, points at him, confirming that there is no possible doubt and that it is definitely their Duke.

56 - Hic Franci pugnant et ceciderunt qui eram cum Haroldo (Here, the French fight, and those who were with Harold die).

Reassured that their leader is safe, the French have found courage agin and re-entered the battle with new ardour, pursuing the English whom they compel to leave their entrenchments and fight in open ground. All fight mercilessly in deadly hand to hand combat: heads fly under the sword blows, mutilated copses litter the ground. William then gives orders to his archers, who have been well-provided with reserves of arrows, commanding them to fire high to avoid their arrows falling uselessly on the leather shields.

Scene 55

57 - Hic Harold rex interfectus est (Here, King Harold is killed).

The Saxon foot-soldiers are literally cut to pieces. However, at the top of the hill, the elite troops, the famous house-carls, are still resisting, in square formation around the King and his "dragon" standard. It is at this moment that a Norman arrow, shot by some unknown archer whose name remains unknown to history, hits Harold in the right eye with such violence that it penetrates right into the skull. He tries in vain to pull it out, but dies, finished off by a Norman horseman. King Harold is dead.

58 - Et fuga verterunt Angli (And the English fled).

The death of their leader causes the English to rout. They cease to resist these terrifying Norman horsemen mad with victory and, in the closing light of day, they flee the bloody battlefield. These are the pictures (heavily restored) with which, as far as we are concerned, the Tapestry closes. On the evening of 14 October 1066, William, the victor at Hastings, enters gloriously into History.

cene 57

An unfinished story

Drawings made in the 18th century show the Tapestry to have already been damaged. It is difficult to estimate the length of the missing part. Probably only a few scenes have disappeared. One can imagine the end of the story might have been the Coronation of William in Westminster Abbey on Christmas Day, 1066.

30

The year 1066

5 January: Death of Edward the Confessor.
6 January: Coronation of Harold.
September: The Norman fleet assembles at Dives then at Saint-Valéry-sur-Somme.
Invasion of England by Harald Hardrada, King of Norway, supported by Harold's brother, Tostig.
25 September: Battle of Stamford Bridge. Victory of Harold over the Norwegians.
28 September: the Normans land at Pevensey.
29 September: William establishes his camp at Hastings.
6 October: Harold and his troops reach London.
14 October: Battle of Hastings.
Death of Harold.
21 October: Dover surrenders.
29 October: Canterbury surrenders.
25 December: Coronation of William at Westminster.

The theatre of operations

Scene 23 brings the two claimants to the throne of England face to face William on the left and Harold in the centre.

The Tapestry through the centuries

The Tapestry survived many dangerous situations while it belonged to the Cathedral Treasury: fires in the 12th century, the destruction and pillaging of the Hundred Years' War, the Wars of Religion and the Revolution. It left Bayeux for the first time in November 1803, at the request of Bonaparte, so that it could be exhibited at the Louvre. Entrusted on its return to the care of the townspeople of Bayeux, it has been on permanent display since 1842, with the exception of the period of the Second World War, when it was stored for safety at the Château de Sourches (Sarthe). After a short stay at the Louvre, it returned to Bayeux in March 1945. It is to be found today in the former Great Seminary, a vast building dating from the 17th century.

The Museum of the Bayeux Tapestry is housed in the former Great Seminary in Bayeux.
(Photo: Municipal Library, Bayeux).

Practical information

Museum address
Centre Guillaume-le-Conquérant,
rue de Nesmond, 14400 Bayeux
Tel: 02 31.92.05.48
Fax: 02 31.92.06.41

Opening times
The Bayeux Tapestry can be seen every day of the year except 25 December and 1st January.

From 1st to 15 September, it is open all day from 9 am to 7 pm without a break.
Last admission: for the whole museum, one hour before closing and for the Tapestry only, thirty minutes before closing.

Optional earphone hire.

Layout of the museum
You are advised to follow the route indicated by arrows.
On the 1st floor: an audio-visual display about the Vikings; explanatory panels on the Tapestry; models, figures, maps on life in England under William's rule.
On the 2nd floor: a film presentation, in French or English, relating the story of the Conquest of England.
(It is advisable to ascertain the times at reception.)

On the ground floor: the Tapestry.
(Optional earphone hire, with commentary in either French or German, English, Italian, Japanese or Dutch.)

Front cover:
Scene 23. Harold's oath
Back cover:
Detail of scene 12.
Front and back flyleaves:
Scene 48. William's cavalry

❶ Tourist Office Pont-Saint-Jean. Tél : 02 31 92 16 26
❷ William the Conquerc Centre, Rue de Nesmonc (Bayeux Tapestry) Tél : 02 31 92 05 48
❸ Cathedral of Notre-Dame
❹ Baron Gérard Museur Place de la Liberté. Tél : 02 31 92 14 21
❺ Memorial Museum o the Battle of Normandy, 1944. Tél : 02 31 92 93 4
❻ Diocesan Museum of Religious Art and Conser vatory of Bayeux LACE Hôtel du Doyen. Tél : 02 31 92 73 80
❼ Memorial Museum « Général de Gaulle and Bayeux ».
❽ British Military cemetery and memorial

I.S.B.N. 2.7373.2064.X - Dépôt légal : juin 1996 - N° d'éditeur 3453.03.06.03.01
Cet ouvrage a été achevé d'imprimer par Fournier A.Graphicas, S.A.Victoria.

AD PRE